THE WORLD'S 60 BEST SALADS... PERIOD.
VÉRONIQUE PARADIS

PHOTOGRAPHER: Antoine Sicotte
ART DIRECTOR: Antoine Sicotte
GRAPHIC DESIGNER: Laurie Auger
COVER DESIGNER: Laurie Auger
FOOD STYLIST: Véronique Paradis
ENGLISH TRANSLATOR: Lorien Jones
COPY EDITOR: Emily Raine

PROJECT EDITOR: Antoine Ross Trempe

ISBN: 978-2-920943-53-7

©2012, CARDINAL PUBLISHERS / LES ÉDITIONS CARDINAL
All rights reserved.

Legal Deposit: 2012
Bibliothèque et Archives du Québec
Library and Archives Canada
ISBN : 978-2-920943-53-7

The publisher acknowledges the financial support of the Government of Canada through the Canada Book Fund (CBF) for its publishing activities and the support of the Government of Quebec through the tax credits for book publishing program (SODEC).

Originally published under the title *"Les 60 meilleures salades du monde... Point final."*

PRINTED IN CANADA

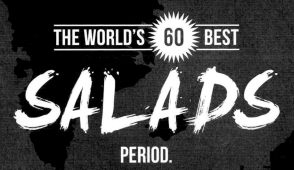

THE WORLD'S 60 BEST

SALADS

PERIOD.

THE WORLD'S 60 BEST

SALADS

PERIOD.

ABOUT THIS BOOK

The 60 salads in this book are, *in our opinion*, the 60 best salads in the world. Our team of chefs, writers and gourmets explored everything the culinary world has to offer to create this collection of the world's 60 best salads.

We based our recipes on the following criteria:

QUALITY OF INGREDIENTS
ORIGINALITY
TASTE
APPEARANCE
SIMPLICITY

Are these our personal favorite dishes? Of course! But rest assured, our team of passionate, dedicated gourmets put time and loving care into formulating and testing each recipe in order to provide you with the 60 best salads ever. In fact, our chef brought each freshly made salad straight from the kitchen into the studio—no colorants, no sprays, no special effects added—and after each photo shoot, our creative team happily devoured the very salads you see in the photos.

We hope you'll enjoy discovering these recipes and using this book as much as we enjoyed making it.

TABLE OF CONTENTS

INTRO

Every one of the 60 best recipes in this book features a flavor and cost legend (see pages 018 and 019) to guide your taste buds as well as your wallet in choosing the perfect dish. You will also find a glossary of culinary terms (page 029), handy cooking tips and tricks (page 025), and a list of must-have kitchen tools (page 023) that will help you create the world's BEST recipes. Finally, use the easy-to-follow Table of Contents (pages 010 and 011) and Ingredients Index (pages 176 to 181) to find everything you're looking for.

Impress guests with your food knowledge from our informative "Did you know?" sidebars, and take your meals to the next level thanks to our tasty tips and serving suggestions!

Bon appétit!

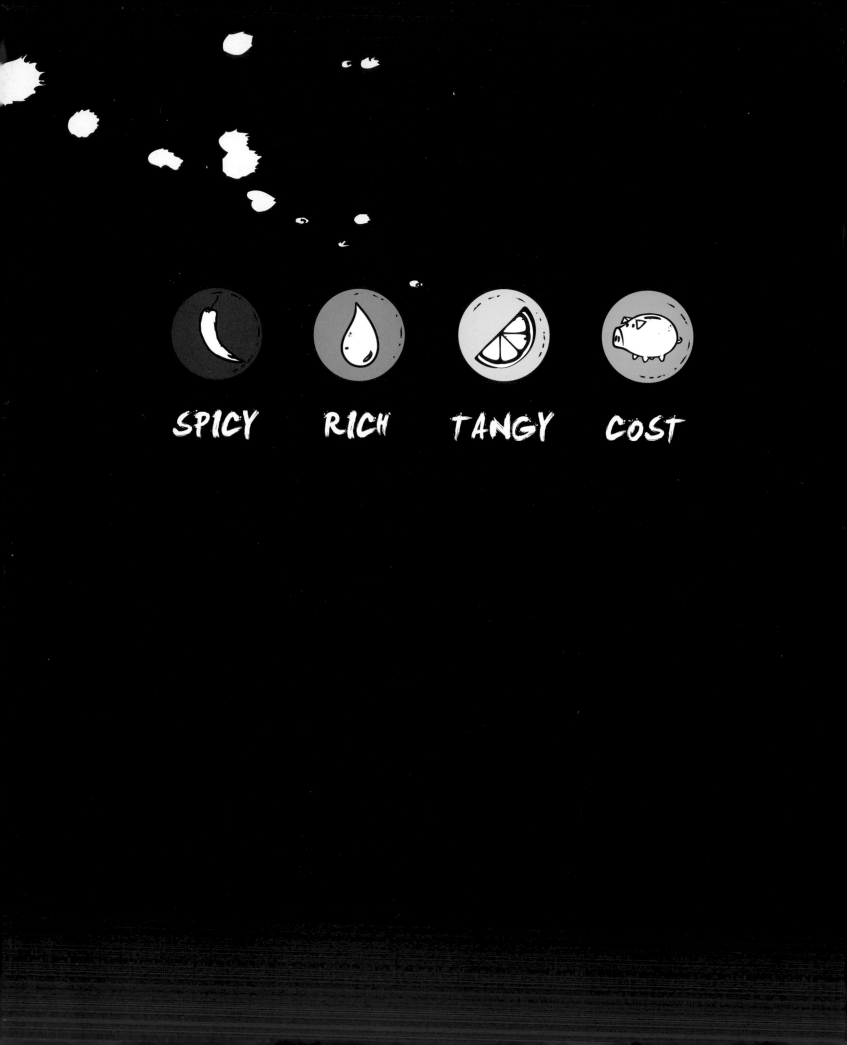

SPICY   RICH   TANGY   COST

LEGEND

HOT • PEPPERY • ZESTY

LOW   MEDIUM   HIGH

CREAMY • BUTTERY • LUSCIOUS

LOW   MEDIUM   HIGH

ACIDIC • LEMONY • VINEGARY

LOW   MEDIUM   HIGH

COST OF INGREDIENTS

LOW   MEDIUM   HIGH

A SHORT HISTORY OF THE SALAD

The English word *salad* first appeared around the 14th century, and comes from the Latin word *sal*, which means salt. The ancient Romans, Greeks, and Egyptians were great lovers of salads, especially with salted dressings. Nowadays, the most popular and recognizable salads contain leafy vegetables such as romaine, chicory, arugula, mâche, or plain iceberg lettuce. But—as you'll find out in this book—there's more to salad than just green leaves. Salads are wonderfully versatile, and can include anything from raw or cooked vegetables to meat, eggs, or seafood. Paired with a flavorful vinaigrette or dressing, this delicious dish deserves to be a meal's main attraction.

Every country has its own traditional salad recipe. Caesar salad and Waldorf salad were first made popular in America. Liège salade originated in Belgium, fattoush salad in Lebanon, niçoise in France, mechouia in Tunisia, and olivier salad in Russia. A typical Mexican salad might be made with corn, black beans, cucumber, and cumin, while the world-famous Greek salad is composed of tangy feta cheese and fresh vegetables.

Salads offer a marvelous medley of colors, flavors, and textures. A salad can be simple, sophisticated, seasonal, exotic, or a spur-of-the-moment bowlful of whatever's left over in the refrigerator.

So sharpen your knives and get chopping—it's salad time!

MUST-HAVE TOOLS

WHAT YOU NEED TO MAKE THE WORLD'S BEST SALADS.

1. A **whisk** for vinaigrettes and dressings

2. A **large salad bowl** for mixing salads

3. A **small glass** or **stainless steel bowl** for mixing vinaigrettes and dressings (never use a plastic bowl!)

4. A **hand blender** for making pesto or for easy mixing

5. Large **salad tongs** or **wooden spoons** for tossing salads

6. A **large frying pan** for cooking

7. A **chef's knife** for chopping, cubing, dicing and mincing

8. A **large pot** for blanching

9. A **mandoline** for perfectly julienned vegetables

10. A **zester** or small grater for zesting citrus fruits

TIPS & TRICKS

FOR CREATING THE WORLD'S BEST SALADS

1. The key to making the best salads is using only the freshest ingredients.

2. Salad isn't just a side dish—it can be a full-blown main course or even dessert. However you serve it, salad deserves as much love and careful preparation as any other dish.

3. The very best salad has the very best vinaigrette.

4. Salad is so much more than just plain old lettuce!

5. It's important to toss a salad with its vinaigrette at exactly the right moment, and to mix it gently to avoid crushing the ingredients.

6. Yes, you can put meat in your salad.

7. The beauty of salad is that there are no rules—let this book inspire you to create YOUR best salad!

8. Because they require little to no cooking, salads make the perfect summer meal and are great for picnics, lunches, or even a light snack.

9. The best salads are inspired by culinary traditions from across the globe.

10. With salad, anything goes! Use a plate, a bowl, or even a cup, and dig in with your fingers, your hands, or the usual utensils.

HOW-TO GUIDE

THE SECRET TO MAKING THE PERFECT EMULSION

An emulsion is a mixture of two or more liquids that normally can't be combined. To prevent the liquids from separating, an emulsifier must be added. The combination of vinegar and oil is a classic example of an emulsion that would quickly separate if an emulsifier, like egg yolk or mustard, weren't added.

The most distinct characteristic of emulsion sauces is their instability or tendency to separate. Preparing an emulsion requires careful attention to technique—even the slightest misstep could result in a ruined sauce.

1. Make sure ingredients have been thoroughly mixed BEFORE adding oil;

2. Make sure oil is at room temperature before incorporating in a slow, steady stream.

BASIC EMULSION TIPS

MAYONNAISE
Making mayonnaise requires continuous and vigorous whisking while adding oil in a slow steady stream to a mixture of egg yolk, mustard, vinegar, and seasoning. Adding the oil too quickly OR too slowly or adding oil that is too cold may cause mayonnaise to separate, or "break." Store mayonnaise in a covered jar or container in the refrigerator.

VINAIGRETTE
Vinaigrette is an unstable or temporary emulsion, which means that the components will quickly separate after being mixed together. Vinaigrette can be served as is, or an emulsifier (like egg yolk) can be added to stabilize the emulsion and prevent separation. Store vinaigrette in a covered bottle or container in the refrigerator.

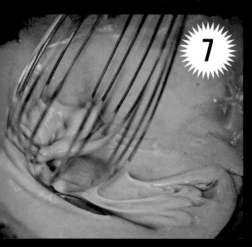

GLOSSARY

1. SEASON

To improve the flavor of a dish by adding salt and pepper to taste.

2. BLANCH

To cook vegetables briefly in boiling salted water.

3. BRUNOISE

A basic knife cut in which food is cut into very small cubes, about 1/8 inch.

4. DICE

A basic knife cut in which food is cut into cubes.

5. DEGLAZE

To remove and dissolve caramelized bits of food at the bottom of a pan in order to make a jus or a sauce.

6. THINLY SLICE

To cut into thin, equal slices.

7. EMULSION

A mixture of two or more liquids or substances that normally can't be combined. An emulsifier such as egg yolk or mustard is often added to prevent separation.

8. CHOP

To cut into small pieces with a sharp instrument (knife or food processor).

9. REDUCE

To thicken a liquid by evaporation over heat.

10. JULIENNE

A basic knife cut in which food is cut into long thin strips. A mandoline is often used for this cut.

11. SEAR

To cook in fat (butter or oil) at a high temperature to obtain a golden or brown crust.

12. ZEST

To remove the zest (outer skin) of citrus fruits with a zester, grater, or peeling knife.

THE CHEF'S SECRET

Every seasoned chef will attest that the real secret to creating a successful dish is to *taste! taste! taste!* Taste before and after seasoning, add some heat or a squeeze of lemon juice if you think your dish needs a little kick, or go ahead and double the herbs or even the cheese! The most important thing is to follow your instincts and your senses. Listen for that telltale sizzle, inhale the tantalizing aromas, and CONSTANTLY taste your food so you can get to know your dish in all its stages.

There you have it the simple secret to creating delicious, original dishes.

FUNKY FIJIAN SALAD

SERVES 4

DID YOU KNOW?

Kokoda is a Fijian version of ceviche, a seafood dish popular across Latin America made with raw fish or seafood marinated in lime juice. The lime's acidity cooks the fish until no longer translucent.

FOR SALAD

2 fillets fresh firm white fish (halibut or tilapia),
cut into 3/4 -inch cubes
1/2 cup (125 ml) lime juice
1/4 cup (60 ml) thick coconut milk
1/2 red onion, finely chopped
1/2 cup (125 ml) cilantro, roughly chopped
1 jalapeño pepper, seeded and finely chopped
1/2 cup (125 ml) fresh corn kernels
Salt and freshly ground pepper

PREPARATION

Combine fish and lime juice. Refrigerate for 3 hours.

Drain fish and add all other ingredients. Mix well. Season with salt and pepper. Chill for 1 hour before serving.

BLÜE ENDIVE

SERVES 4

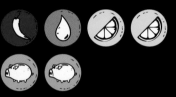

FOR SALAD

3 endives
1 pear
1/2 cup (125 ml) red grapes, halved
1/2 cup (125 ml) walnuts, toasted and roughly chopped
1/2 cup (125 ml) blue cheese, crumbled

FOR VINAIGRETTE

2 tbsp white wine vinegar
1 tsp Dijon mustard
1 tsp honey
1 shallot, minced
1/4 cup (60 ml) olive oil

PREPARATION

Cut endives in half and remove hearts. Slice lengthwise into very thin strips. Using a mandoline, julienne the pear. Combine all salad ingredients.

In a bowl, whisk together vinegar, mustard, honey and shallot. Add oil in a slow steady stream.

Toss salad with vinaigrette and serve.

 **DID YOU KNOW?**

To prevent cut pears from turning brown, soak them in lemon water for a few minutes or until it's time to put the salad together.

DECADENT POTATO SALAD

SERVES 4

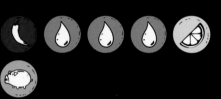

FOR SALAD

3 white-fleshed potatoes, unpeeled and cut into large cubes
3 hard-boiled eggs, quartered
1 cup (250 ml) vegetable oil
3 shallots, minced
4 slices bacon, cut into 2 cm pieces
1/4 cup (60 ml) chopped chives

FOR DRESSING

1 egg yolk
1 tbsp lemon juice
1 tbsp Dijon mustard
1 clove garlic, minced
1/2 cup (125 ml) vegetable oil
5 drops Tabasco sauce
Salt and freshly ground pepper
1 tbsp wholegrain mustard

PREPARATION

Fill a pot with water. Add potatoes and salt and bring to a boil. Cook for 10 minutes or until potatoes are tender and easily pierced with a knife.

Heat oil in a deep sauté pan. Fry shallots until golden brown, remove from heat, and pat dry to remove excess oil. Cook bacon in a frying pan and set aside.

In a bowl, prepare dressing by whisking together the egg yolk, lemon juice, mustard and garlic for 2 minutes. Add oil in a steady stream, whisking vigorously until mixture has reached the consistency of mayonnaise. Add Tabasco sauce, salt, pepper, and wholegrain mustard.

In a salad bowl, combine potatoes, bacon, chives and dressing. Add eggs and shallots and gently mix. Season and serve.

TASTY TIP

Why not add cubes of sharp cheddar cheese to give your salad a little zing?

ROBUST RASPBERRY SALAD

SERVES 4

FOR SALAD

1 tbsp olive oil
8 chicken livers, cleaned
1/2 cup (125 ml) red onion, finely chopped
1/2 cup (125 ml) fresh raspberries
2 tbsp red wine
2 tbsp raspberry vinegar
2 tbsp butter
1/4 cup (60 ml) toasted sliced almonds
2 tbsp parsley, chopped
2 cups (500 ml) baby spinach

PREPARATION

Heat olive oil in a very hot non-stick pan. Brown chicken livers for 1 minute on each side. Add red onion and raspberries and cook for 1 minute. Deglaze with red wine, then add raspberry vinegar and butter. When butter is melted, sprinkle in almonds and parsley. Remove from heat and serve on a bed of baby spinach.

TASTY TIP

Kick it up a notch by adding some creamy goat cheese!

MEXICAN SALAD

SERVES 4

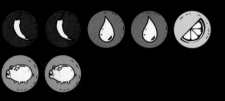

FOR SHRIMP

1 tbsp canola oil
2 corn tortillas
1 cup (250 ml) Nordic shrimp
1/2 cup (125 ml) fresh corn kernels
1 red pepper, julienned
1 avocado, peeled and diced
3 tomatoes, diced
1 handful fresh cilantro, washed and roughly chopped
Salt and freshly ground pepper to taste

FOR VINAIGRETTE

1 shallot, peeled
2 jalapeño peppers, halved and seeded
1 tbsp Dijon mustard
1/4 cup (60 ml) sherry vinegar
1/2 an egg yolk
1/2 cup (125 ml) canola oil
Salt and freshly ground pepper to taste

PREPARATION

Brush corn tortillas with oil. Cut into halves and then into 1/4 -inch strips. Spread strips in a single layer on a baking sheet and cook for 10 minutes at 350°F (180°C) or until golden brown and crisp. In a salad bowl, combine all shrimp ingredients except tortilla strips.

Sauté shallot and jalapeños in a small saucepan. With a hand blender or in a food processor, purée shallot, jalapeños, mustard, sherry vinegar and egg yolk. Add oil in a steady stream, blending until fully incorporated and smooth. Add salt and pepper.

Pour vinaigrette over shrimp mixture and toss to coat. Add tortilla strips and toss again. Serve.

SMOKED DUCK SALAD BOATS

SERVES 4

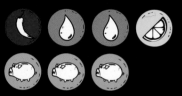

FOR SALAD

2 endives, whole leaves, hearts removed
Seeds from 1/2 pomegranate
8 slices smoked duck, cut into small pieces
3 fresh dates, pitted and diced
80 g fresh goat cheese

FOR POMEGRANATE VINAIGRETTE

1 shallot, minced
2 tbsp sherry vinegar
1/2 cup (125 ml) canola oil
2 tbsp Dijon mustard
2 tbsp pomegranate juice, strained
1/2 tsp ground allspice
Salt and freshly ground pepper

PREPARATION

Arrange endive leaves on a serving platter. Combine pomegranate seeds, smoked duck, dates, and goat cheese, divide into equal portions and fill endive leaves.

In a bowl, combine vinaigrette ingredients. Drizzle over each endive leaf. Serve.

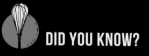

DID YOU KNOW?

Both professional and amateur chefs love endive because it's so easy to prepare!

TOMATO MOZZA PESTO

SERVES 4

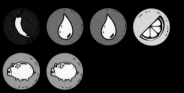

FOR SALAD

1 ball fresh mozzarella cheese
1 tbsp fresh oregano, chopped
2 tbsp white balsamic vinegar
2 tbsp olive oil
3 medium tomatoes
Sea salt
Freshly ground pepper

FOR PESTO

1/2 cup (125 ml) fresh basil
1 clove garlic
1 tbsp fresh Parmesan cheese, grated
1 tbsp pine nuts
1/4 cup (60 ml) olive oil

PREPARATION

Drain mozzarella and cut into 1/2-inch slices. In a bowl, combine oregano, vinegar and oil. Add cheese and marinate for 30 minutes. Cut tomatoes into 1/2-inch slices.

With a hand blender or in a food processor, purée basil, garlic, Parmesan cheese and pine nuts. Pour in oil in a steady stream until fully incorporated and smooth.

Arrange alternating tomato and mozzarella slices on a serving platter. Season with sea salt and freshly ground pepper. Drizzle pesto over salad.

LA CAESAR

SERVES 4

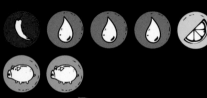

FOR SALAD

1/4 cup (60 ml) olive oil
2 cloves garlic, crushed
4 slices bread, cubed
1 cup (250 ml) bacon
1 head romaine lettuce, torn into bite-sized pieces
1/4 cup (60 ml) fresh Parmesan cheese shavings
Freshly ground pepper

FOR CAESAR DRESSING

1 egg yolk
1 tbsp lemon juice
1 tbsp Dijon mustard
1 clove garlic, minced
2 anchovy fillets, mashed
3/4 cup (180 ml) vegetable oil
2 tbsp capers, minced
1/2 cup (125 ml) fresh Parmesan cheese, grated

PREPARATION

In a bowl, prepare dressing by whisking together the egg yolk, lemon juice, mustard, garlic and anchovies. Pour in oil in a steady stream, whisking vigorously until mixture is creamy. Add capers and Parmesan cheese. Refrigerate for 1 hour.

Heat olive oil with both crushed garlic cloves, cooking until golden, then discard garlic. Fry bread cubes in garlic oil until golden brown. Remove and reserve croutons. In the same pan, cook bacon until crisp. Drain bacon on paper towels and roughly chop. Set aside.

In a salad bowl, toss romaine lettuce, bacon and croutons with dressing. Garnish with Parmesan shavings and season with freshly ground pepper.

STRAWBERRY PISTACHIO MASCARPONE

SERVES 4

FOR SALAD

2 cups (500 ml) fresh strawberries, hulled and halved
2 tbsp blackcurrant liqueur
1 tbsp icing sugar
1 tbsp lemon juice
1/4 cup (60 ml) fresh mint, chopped

FOR PISTACHIO CREAM

1/2 cup (125 ml) pistachios
2 squares white baking chocolate
1 1/2 tbsp lemon juice
2 tbsp icing sugar
3 tbsp mascarpone cheese
2 tbsp water

PREPARATION

In a bowl, combine strawberries with blackcurrant liqueur, icing sugar and lemon juice and let stand 30 minutes.

With a hand blender or in a food processor, blend pistachios, white chocolate, lemon juice and icing sugar until smooth, and then add mascarpone and water.

Spoon strawberries into attractive bowls, add a dollop of pistachio cream to each, and garnish with mint.

FRESH TUNA NIÇOISE

SERVES 4

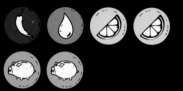

FOR SALAD

2 small fresh tuna steaks
Salt and freshly ground pepper
1 handful (about 20) green beans, blanched and cut in half
4 hard-boiled eggs, quartered
2 tomatoes, quartered
8 new potatoes, blanched and quartered
1/2 red onion, finely chopped
12 black olives, pitted
8 leaves romaine lettuce, torn into bite-sized pieces

FOR VINAIGRETTE

6 anchovy fillets, mashed
2 cloves garlic, crushed and minced
2 tbsp white balsamic vinegar
1 tsp Dijon mustard
1/3 cup (80 ml) olive oil
Freshly ground pepper

PREPARATION

Season tuna with salt and pepper. Heat oil in a very hot skillet and sear tuna for 15 seconds per side. Tuna should still be pink inside. Remove from pan and thinly slice.

In a bowl, combine anchovies, garlic, vinegar and mustard. While whisking, pour in oil in a steady stream. Add pepper.

To assemble the salad, combine vegetables in a salad bowl, dress with vinaigrette, and toss well.

Top with sliced tuna and quartered eggs. Add another splash of vinaigrette and serve.

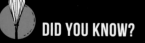

DID YOU KNOW?

The secret to perfect hard-boiled eggs? Never cook for more than 11 minutes after the water comes to a boil, otherwise the yolk will have a green "crust" and the white will be unpleasantly rubbery.

LORD LOBSTER & LADY SALAD

SERVES 4

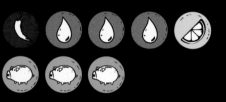

FOR SALAD

1/2 cup (125 ml) orzo
2 whole lobsters, cooked
1/2 cup (125 ml) green peas
1/4 radicchio, thinly sliced

FOR DRESSING

1 egg yolk
Zest and juice of 1 lemon
2 lobster tomalleys (the soft, green substance found inside the lobster)
1 tbsp Dijon mustard
1/2 cup (125 ml) vegetable oil
Salt and freshly ground pepper

PREPARATION

In a pot, add orzo to salted water and bring to a boil. Drain and chill.

Shell cooked lobster. Cut tail meat into large pieces. Pull out pincer meat, keeping it whole, and set aside. Remove tomalleys and reserve for dressing.

In a bowl, whisk together the egg yolk, tomalleys, lemon juice and zest, and mustard. Add oil in a steady stream, whisking vigorously until mixture is smooth. Season with salt and pepper.

In a salad bowl, toss orzo, lobster tail meat, green peas, and radicchio with dressing. Plate salad and top with pincer meat.

 **DID YOU KNOW?**

Atlantic lobster season typically begins in May. For 9 weeks lobster fishermen head offshore before dawn, haul up the traps and bring the day's catch back to shore in the afternoon to prepare for the next day.

12

MANGO CHICKEN SALAD

SERVES 4

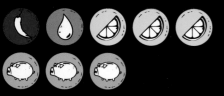

FOR MARINADE

1/4 cup (60 ml) sweet Thai chili sauce
2 cloves garlic, crushed
1 kaffir lime, juice, zest and leaves (leaves optional)
1 onion, chopped
2 tbsp vegetable oil

FOR SALAD

2 chicken breasts, cut in half lengthwise
1/2 cup (125 ml) unsweetened shredded coconut
1/4 cup (60 ml) bread crumbs
1/4 cup (60 ml) all-purpose flour
1 egg
1/4 cup (60 ml) canola oil
1 fresh mango, cubed
1/2 cup (125 ml) fresh cilantro
1/2 cup (125 ml) red onion, finely chopped
A few chicory leaves
A few frisée leaves

FOR VINAIGRETTE

1/4 cup (60 ml) mango juice
2 tbsp lime juice
2 tbsp dark rum
1/4 cup (60 ml) extra virgin olive oil
1 tsp Dijon mustard
Salt and freshly ground pepper

PREPARATION

Combine all marinade ingredients. Add chicken and marinate for 2 hours.

In a bowl, mix together coconut and bread crumbs. Coat marinated chicken with flour, dip in egg, and dredge in coconut and bread crumb mixture. Heat oil in a pan and fry chicken for 3 to 4 minutes on each side until fully cooked and coating is crispy. If pieces are not fully cooked through, finish in the oven at 350°F (180°C).

In a large bowl, combine mango, cilantro, onion, chicory and lettuce.

Whisk together vinaigrette ingredients, pouring in oil in a steady stream.

Toss salad with vinaigrette. Arrange chicken over salad on a serving plate.

 **TASTY TIP**

Try this salad with shrimp instead of chicken!

BEETS WITH TARRAGON PESTO

SERVES 4

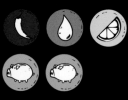

FOR SALAD

3 medium beets
2 tbsp sherry vinegar
2 tbsp olive oil
Salt and freshly ground pepper
1 handful of arugula leaves
1/4 cup (60 ml) almonds, chopped

FOR TARRAGON PESTO

1/4 cup (60 ml) fresh tarragon
1 cup (250 ml) arugula
1/4 cup (60 ml) toasted almonds
2 tbsp fresh Parmesan cheese
1 clove garlic
1 tbsp lemon juice
1 tsp honey
1/3 cup (80 ml) olive oil

PREPARATION

Fill a pot with water. Salt water, add beets and bring to a boil. Cook until beets are tender and easily pierced with a knife. Drain and cool, then peel and thinly slice. Toss with sherry vinegar, oil, salt and pepper. Set aside.

With a hand blender or in a food processor, combine all pesto ingredients except the oil. Add oil in a steady stream until pesto is smooth and creamy.

Arrange beet slices on a serving plate. Drizzle with tarragon pesto and garnish with arugula and toasted almonds.

TASTY TIP

Top this salad with fresh or fried goat cheese (see page 120), but you might want to double the recipe – your guests will definitely want seconds!

LEMONY YOGURT RAPINI

SERVES 4

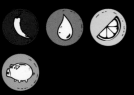

FOR SALAD

1 bunch rapini

FOR LEMON YOGURT SAUCE

1/2 cup (125 ml) Greek yogurt
1 clove garlic, minced
1 tbsp olive oil
Zest and juice of 1 lemon
1 tsp salt
Freshly ground pepper

PREPARATION

Trim tough bases of rapini stalks. Blanch for 2 minutes in a large pot of boiling salted water. Drain and transfer immediately to a bowl of ice water to preserve color.

In a bowl, mix together yogurt sauce ingredients.

Spoon yogurt sauce onto a serving plate and top with rapini.

PUMPED-UP PAPAYA

SERVES 4

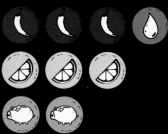

DID YOU KNOW?

Green papaya is slightly tart and peppery and can be eaten plain or with a squeeze of fresh lemon juice.

FOR SALAD

1 lb beef sirloin steak, cut 1/2-inch thick
2 tbsp Thai fish sauce
2 tbsp coarse ground black pepper
1 tbsp olive oil
1 large green papaya, peeled and julienned
4 green onions, thinly sliced
1/2 cucumber, julienned
1/2 cup (125 ml) fresh mint
1/2 cup (125 ml) fresh basil

FOR VINAIGRETTE

1/4 cup (60 ml) lime juice
2 tbsp sugar
1 clove garlic, minced
1/2 hot pepper, seeded and minced
2 tbsp fish sauce

FOR GARNISH

1/4 cup (60 ml) fresh cilantro, chopped
1/4 cup (60 ml) cashew nuts, coarsely chopped
1 tbsp olive oil

PREPARATION

Brush steak with fish sauce and coat with pepper. Sear in a very hot pan in olive oil, about 2 minutes each side. Thinly slice and set aside.

In a bowl, mix together vinaigrette ingredients. In a separate salad bowl, combine papaya, green onion, cucumber, mint and basil. Toss with vinaigrette. Immediately before serving, add beef and garnish with cilantro, cashew nuts, and a splash of olive oil.

CAULIFLOWER, CABBAGE & CREAMY RICOTTA

SERVES 4

FOR SALAD

1 1/2 cups (375 ml) cauliflower, cut into small florets
2 tbsp vegetable oil
1 1/2 cups (375 ml) Chinese cabbage, sliced into very thin ribbons
1 apple, diced
1/3 cup (80 ml) pine nuts, toasted
1/2 cup (125 ml) ricotta cheese

FOR VINAIGRETTE

2 shallots, finely chopped
1 tbsp vegetable oil
1 tsp curry powder
1 sprig thyme
1 bay leaf
1/4 cup (60 ml) white wine
2 tbsp sherry vinegar
1/2 cup (125 ml) canola oil
Juice of 1 lemon

PREPARATION

In a bowl, toss cauliflower with vegetable oil. Spread evenly on a baking sheet and broil for 4 minutes or until golden brown. Set aside.

In a frying pan, sweat shallots in vegetable oil. Add curry, thyme, bay leaf and white wine. Reduce until wine has evaporated. Remove bay leaf. Chill and set aside.

With a hand blender or in a food processor, mix together the cooked shallots and vinegar. Pour in oil in a steady stream then add lemon juice.

In a salad bowl, mix together cauliflower, cabbage, diced apple, pine nuts and vinaigrette. Top with small dollops of ricotta cheese and serve.

TASTY TIP

This salad pairs perfectly with pan-fried trout!

AUTHENTIC FATTOUSH

SERVES 4

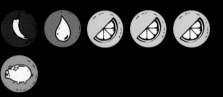

FOR SALAD

1 bunch mâche (also called corn salad or lamb's lettuce)
1 bunch fresh mint
1 bunch fresh flat-leaf parsley
10 cherry tomatoes, halved
1/2 cucumber, diced
3 radishes, finely chopped
1 onion, finely chopped

FOR VINAIGRETTE

1 clove garlic, minced
Juice of 1 lemon
Salt and freshly ground pepper
1/4 cup (60 ml) olive oil
1 pinch sumac

FOR GARNISH

1/4 cup (60 ml) labneh (or fresh cheese)
1 Lebanese pita, toasted and cut into slices

PREPARATION

In a small bowl, mix together vinaigrette ingredients. Combine all salad ingredients in a salad bowl. Toss with vinaigrette. Top with labneh and serve with sliced pita.

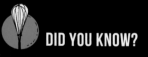 **DID YOU KNOW?**

Labneh is a soft, slightly tart fresh cheese made from yogurt.

CUMIN-ROASTED JERUSALEM ARTICHOKES

SERVES 4

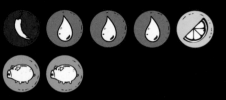

FOR SALAD

1 leek, cut into 1/2-inch pieces
4 cups Jerusalem artichokes, washed and chopped
into 1/2-inch cubes
4 cups new potatoes, halved
1 tbsp butter
1 tbsp vegetable oil
Salt and freshly ground pepper
4 cups celery leaves (or baby spinach), washed

FOR CUMIN MAYONNAISE

1 egg yolk
2 tbsp wholegrain mustard
Juice of 1/2 lemon
1 tsp ground cumin
Salt and freshly ground pepper
1/2 cup (125 ml) vegetable oil

PREPARATION

Evenly spread leek, Jerusalem artichokes and potatoes in one layer on a baking sheet covered in parchment paper. Cut butter into small pieces and distribute over vegetables, then drizzle with oil. Cook in a 400°F (200°C) for 30 minutes or until vegetables are easily pierced with a knife. Let cool.

In a bowl, prepare mayonnaise by whisking together the egg yolk, mustard, lemon juice, cumin, salt and pepper for 2 minutes. Add oil in a steady stream and whisk vigorously until mixture becomes creamy.

In a salad bowl, toss roasted vegetables with celery leaves and mayonnaise. Serve.

SUNNY TABBOULEH

SERVES 4

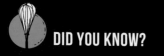

FOR SALAD

1 tbsp olive oil
1/3 cup (80 ml) bulgur
1 cup (250 ml) water
2 cups (500 ml) fresh parsley leaves, finely chopped
1/2 cup (125 ml) fresh mint, finely chopped
3 green onions, finely chopped
2 medium tomatoes, seeded and diced

FOR VINAIGRETTE

1/3 cup (80 ml) extra virgin olive oil
Zest and juice of 1 lemon
Salt and freshly ground pepper

PREPARATION

In a pot, heat olive oil and cook bulgur for 1 minute, but don't let it brown. Add water and lower heat. Cook 10 minutes or until water has been fully absorbed. Remove from heat and cover with a cloth and a lid. Let sit for 10 minutes. Fluff with a fork to separate grains. Chill in refrigerator.

In a salad bowl, combine cooled bulgur with remaining salad ingredients. Toss with olive oil, lemon juice, and lemon zest. Season and serve.

DID YOU KNOW?

The word bulgur comes from the Turkish "bulgur," and is also known as bulghur, burghul or bulgar.

GREEK VILLAGE SALAD

SERVES 4

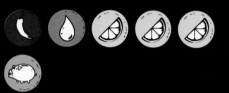

FOR SALAD

2 tomatoes, sliced into rounds
Pinch of sea salt
1/2 cucumber, sliced into rounds
1 red onion, sliced into rounds
16 Kalamata olives
2 tbsp oregano, chopped
1/4 cup (60 ml) olive oil
2 tbsp red wine vinegar
Freshly ground pepper
4 pieces feta cheese, cubed or crumbled

PREPARATION

In a bowl, mix together tomatoes and salt and let sit for 10 minutes. Add cucumber, onion, olives, and oregano. Pour in oil and vinegar, reserving a small amount of each.

Spoon salad onto a serving platter and top with feta cheese. Drizzle with remaining oil and vinegar.

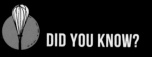

DID YOU KNOW?

The secret to making the tastiest Greek salad is always using the freshest ingredients!

INSALATA DI CALAMARI

SERVES 4

FOR MARINADE

Juice of 1 lemon
1 tbsp olive oil
1 onion, chopped
1 tsp hot pepper paste (or harissa)
2 tbsp white wine

FOR CROUTONS

1/4 baguette, cut into 1-inch cubes
1 tbsp butter

FOR SALAD

4 whole squids, cleaned and cut into 1/2-inch rings
1 tbsp olive oil
2 zucchinis, cut into 1/4-inch rounds

FOR VINAIGRETTE

1 tbsp garlic, minced
Juice of 1 lemon
2 tbsp butter
1/2 tsp harissa
2 tbsp fresh parsley, chopped
1/4 cup (60 ml) water

PREPARATION

Combine all marinade ingredients and pour over squid. Marinate for 1 hour.

In a pan, melt butter. Add croutons and coat with butter, frying until all sides are golden brown. Set aside. In the same pan, heat 1 tbsp olive oil and cook zucchini until golden. Set aside.

Remove squid from marinade. Heat the pan used for croutons and zucchini to a very high temperature, sear squid for 1 minute, and then add garlic, lemon juice, butter, harissa, parsley and water. Remove from heat. In a salad bowl, toss salad ingredients with croutons and zucchini. Serve immediately.

HONEY MUSTARD CHICKEN SALAD

SERVES 4

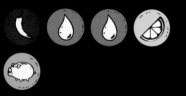

FOR MARINADE

1/4 cup (60 ml) olive oil
2 tbsp lemon juice
5 tbsp (75 ml) honey
1 tbsp Dijon mustard
1 tbsp white wine
1 shallot, minced
1 clove garlic, minced
1 tbsp steak spice
Salt and freshly ground pepper

FOR SALAD

2 chicken breasts
8 leaves frisée lettuce
1 avocado, cubed
16 cherry tomatoes, halved
16 green or yellow beans, blanched
2 green onions, thinly sliced

FOR HONEY MUSTARD DRESSING

1/4 cup (60 ml) mayonnaise (homemade or store-bought)
1 tbsp wholegrain mustard
1 tbsp honey
3 drops Tabasco sauce

PREPARATION

Combine all marinade ingredients and coat chicken breasts with mixture. Marinate for 2 hours.

Cook chicken on the barbecue or in a 350°F (180°C) oven for 20 minutes and then thinly slice. Whisk together all dressing ingredients.

Toss salad ingredients with dressing. On a serving plate, arrange chicken strips on a bed of salad.

23

MELLOW AUTUMN SALAD

SERVES 4

FOR SALAD

2 tbsp butter
2 tbsp olive oil
12 Brussels sprouts, washed and cut in half lengthwise
1 sweet potato, peeled and cubed
2 cloves garlic, chopped
5 sprigs thyme
5 slices bacon, cut into 1-inch pieces
2 red apples, cubed
1/4 cup (60 ml) parsley, chopped

FOR VINAIGRETTE

2 tbsp cider vinegar
1 tsp Dijon mustard
1/4 cup (60 ml) olive oil
Salt and freshly ground pepper

PREPARATION

In a bowl, combine butter and oil with Brussels sprouts, cubed sweet potato, garlic and thyme. Spread mixture onto a baking sheet, with the cut sides of the sprouts facing down. Cook for 30 minutes in a 400°F (200°C) oven or until sprouts and sweet potatoes are easily pierced with a knife.

Cook bacon in a pan. Reserve 1 tbsp bacon fat.

In a small bowl, mix together all vinaigrette ingredients. In a salad bowl, toss vinaigrette with sprouts and sweet potatoes, bacon and reserved fat, chopped apples and parsley. Serve warm.

DID YOU KNOW?

Sweet potatoes, first cultivated in South America, are said to be the first domesticated plant in the New World.

24

SPIKY GREEN BEANS

SERVES 4

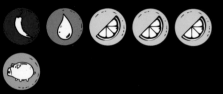

FOR SALAD

4 good handfuls (about 1 lb) green or yellow beans,
whole or sliced in half lengthwise
1/2 cup (125 ml) feta cheese, crumbled
2 shallots, minced
1/2 cup (125 ml) fresh mint, chopped

FOR VINAIGRETTE

2 tbsp lemon juice
1/4 cup (60 ml) olive oil
Salt and freshly ground pepper

PREPARATION

Fill a large pot with water. Add salt and blanch green beans for 1 minute. Drain and transfer immediately to a bowl of ice water to keep beans bright green.

In a salad bowl, combine green beans, feta cheese, shallots and mint. Toss with olive oil and lemon juice. Season and serve.

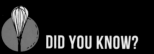

DID YOU KNOW?

Green beans originated in Central and South America, and were introduced into Europe around the 16th century by Spanish explorers returning from the New World. They are now one of the world's most popular vegetables!

25

PRINCESS POTATOES

SERVES 4

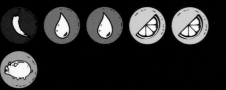

FOR SALAD

2 lbs new potatoes, peeled
1 tbsp olive oil
1 medium onion, finely chopped
1 clove garlic, minced
1 hard-boiled egg, chopped
Zest of 1 lemon
3/4 cup (180 ml) fresh chervil, chopped
Salt and freshly ground pepper

FOR LEMON MAYONNAISE

3/4 cup (180 ml) mayonnaise
Juice of 1 lemon

PREPARATION

With a melon baller, scoop out small balls of potato. Boil in salted water for 10 minutes or until easily pierced with a knife. Drain and allow to cool.

Heat olive oil in a pan. Sauté onion and garlic. In a bowl, combine cooked onion and garlic with chopped hard-boiled egg, lemon zest and chervil. Season with salt and pepper.

In a salad bowl, toss potatoes with mayonnaise and lemon juice, and then roll potatoes in the onion, garlic, egg, zest and chervil mixture. Serve.

26

SAIGON BEEF SALAD

SERVES 4

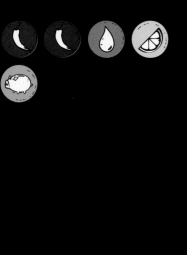

FOR SALAD

1 tbsp vegetable oil
2 sirloin beef steaks (about 1 lb)
1/4 cup (60 ml) steak spice
2 cups (500 ml) arugula
1/2 cup (125 ml) peanuts, toasted and chopped
1/3 cup (80 ml) fresh cilantro leaves
1/3 cup (80 ml) fresh mint leaves
1/3 cup (80 ml) fresh Thai basil leaves
1/2 cup (125 ml) bean sprouts

FOR ASIAN VINAIGRETTE

1 tbsp ginger, chopped
1 tbsp garlic, chopped
1 Thai chili, seeded and chopped
1 tsp sesame oil
1 tbsp honey
1 tbsp Dijon mustard
2 tbsp soy sauce
2 tbsp rice vinegar
1 tsp sriracha sauce (or Asian hot chili sauce)
1/4 cup (60 ml) vegetable oil

PREPARATION

Brush steaks with vegetable oil and coat with steak spice. In a frying pan, grill meat for 2 to 3 minutes each side. Let rest and then thinly slice.

In a bowl, prepare vinaigrette by whisking together all ingredients except oil for 2 minutes. Add oil in a steady stream, whisking vigorously until mixture becomes smooth.

In a salad bowl, combine arugula, peanuts, cilantro, mint, basil and bean sprouts. Add beef slices and vinaigrette. Toss and serve.

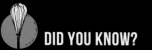

DID YOU KNOW?

Sriracha is a Thai hot sauce, named after the coastal city of Si Racha in Thailand's Chonburi Province. It's made of chili peppers, distilled vinegar, garlic, sugar and salt.

27

ST-VIATEUR SALAD

SERVES 4

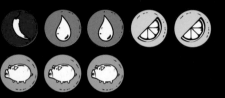

FOR SALAD

1 cup (250 ml) small shell pasta (or other short pasta),
cooked *al dente*
1 avocado, cubed
8 slices smoked salmon, cut into strips
2 tbsp capers, drained and rinsed
4 radishes, julienned
2 cups (500 ml) arugula
1/2 cup (125 ml) fresh dill
Salt and freshly ground pepper

FOR CREAM CHEESE DRESSING

1/4 cup (60 ml) 15% cream
2 tbsp cream cheese
A few drops Tabasco sauce
Zest and juice of 1/2 lemon

PREPARATION

In a bowl, combine cream and cream cheese and microwave
for 30 seconds. Add remaining dressing ingredients, whisking
vigorously until mixture is smooth.

In a salad bowl, mix together all salad ingredients except
arugula and toss with dressing. Add arugula immediately before
serving.

CLASSIC THOUSAND ISLAND

SERVES 4

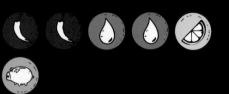

 **DID YOU KNOW?**

Crab cakes are an American specialty composed of crab meat, mayonnaise, eggs, onions, bread crumbs, and seasoning. This mixture is formed into patties and sautéed, baked, or grilled. These tasty morsels are especially popular along the coasts, but can be found in most supermarkets in the frozen foods section!

FOR SALAD

1 head frisée lettuce, torn into bite-sized pieces
12 cherry tomatoes, halved
1/2 cucumber, diced
4 radishes, julienned
A few crab cakes (optional)

FOR THOUSAND ISLAND DRESSING

2 tbsp mayonnaise
2 tbsp orange juice
1/2 tsp paprika
1 tsp Worcestershire
1 tbsp ketchup
1 tbsp sweet pickles, chopped
5 drops Tabasco sauce

PREPARATION

In a small bowl, combine Thousand Island dressing ingredients. In a salad bowl, mix together salad ingredients. Toss with dressing and serve with crab cakes.

VEAL WITH CRISPY ASIAN NOODLES

SERVES 4

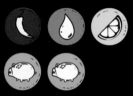

FOR SALAD

1 lb veal steak
Salt and freshly ground pepper
2 cups (500 ml) Chinese cabbage, thinly sliced
1/2 cup (125 ml) bamboo shoots, drained and julienned
1/2 cup (125 ml) snow peas, blanched and julienned
1 1/2 cups (375 ml) ramen-style noodles, broken into pieces

FOR THAI VINAIGRETTE

1/4 cup (60 ml) canola oil
1/4 leek, brunoised
1 clove garlic, minced
1 tbsp ginger, minced
2 tbsp soy sauce
2 tbsp oyster sauce
1 tbsp brown sugar
1 tbsp sesame oil
2 tbsp rice vinegar
2 tbsp black and white sesame seeds, toasted

PREPARATION

Season veal with salt and pepper and grill for 2 minutes on each side. Allow steaks to rest for 5 minutes before thinly slicing.

In a pot, heat 1 tbsp oil. Cook leek, garlic and half of the ginger. Add soy sauce, oyster sauce, brown sugar, sesame oil, remaining canola oil and rice vinegar. Remove from heat and add sesame seeds and remaining ginger. Chill.

In a salad bowl, combine Chinese cabbage, bamboo shoots, snow peas and veal. Toss with vinaigrette. Add noodles immediately before serving.

ANTIPASTO SALAD

SERVES 4

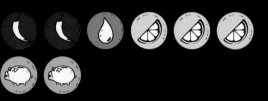

FOR SALAD

2/3 cup (160 ml) canned navy beans, drained and rinsed
1/2 cup (125 ml) hearts of palm, sliced
1/2 cup (125 ml) marinated eggplant
1/3 cup (80 ml) sundried tomatoes, cut into strips
1/2 cup (125 ml) Kalamata olives, pitted
8 slices bresaola (or prosciutto)

FOR VINAIGRETTE

2 tbsp sherry vinegar
1/3 cup (80 ml) olive oil
1/2 tsp crushed red pepper flakes

PREPARATION

In a salad bowl, mix together navy beans, hearts of palm, marinated eggplant, sundried tomatoes and olives. Toss with vinegar, olive oil and crushed red pepper flakes. Let sit for 30 minutes.

Garnish with sliced bresaola immediately before serving.

 **DID YOU KNOW?**

Bresaola is air-dried, salted beef that originated in Italy.

EGG & OYSTER MUSHROOM

SERVES 4

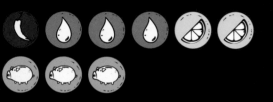

FOR SALAD

8 cups water
1/4 cup (60 ml) white vinegar
4 eggs, poached
1 tbsp butter
4 king oyster mushrooms, thinly sliced
4 slices prosciutto, cubed
4 canned artichoke hearts, sliced
3 cups (750 ml) baby spinach
1 cup (250 ml) radicchio, thinly sliced
Parmesan shavings

FOR TRUFFLE OIL VINAIGRETTE

1 tsp Dijon mustard
1 shallot, minced
1 tbsp sherry vinegar
3 tbsp vegetable oil
1 tbsp truffle oil

PREPARATION

Bring water and vinegar to a boil. Reduce heat. With a spoon, stir the water vigorously to create a whirlpool. One by one, break eggs into water and cook for 4 minutes. Remove with a slotted spoon. Set aside.

To prepare vinaigrette, mix together mustard, shallot and sherry vinegar in a small bowl. Add vegetable oil and then truffle oil in a steady stream.

In a pan, heat butter and cook mushrooms and prosciutto. Add artichokes and remove from heat. Pour vinaigrette over mixture in pan. In a salad bowl, toss mushrooms, prosciutto and artichokes with baby spinach and radicchio. Top with poached eggs and garnish with Parmesan shavings. Serve.

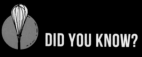

DID YOU KNOW?

What's the science behind poaching an egg? Vinegar causes egg whites to harden more quickly, and breaking eggs into a "whirlpool" allows them to cook in an attractive oval shape.

CRUISE SHIP CRAB & FENNEL

SERVES 4

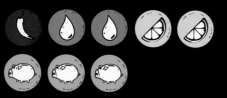

FOR SALAD

1/2 bulb fennel
2 oranges, peeled and sectioned, pith and membranes removed
2 green onions, finely chopped
1 lb fresh crab
1 avocado, thinly sliced

FOR CREAMY ORANGE DRESSING

1 egg yolk
1 tbsp lemon juice
Zest and juice of 1 orange
1 tbsp Dijon mustard
1/2 cup (125 ml) vegetable oil
1 tbsp harissa
Salt and freshly ground pepper

PREPARATION

In a bowl, prepare dressing by whisking together egg yolk, orange juice and zest, and mustard for 2 minutes. Add oil in a steady stream, whisking vigorously until mixture becomes creamy, like a mayonnaise. Add harissa, salt and pepper.

With a mandoline, cut fennel into very thin slices. In a salad bowl, toss fennel, orange sections, green onions, and crab with dressing. Add avocado just a few minutes before serving, mixing gently to keep slices intact.

DID YOU KNOW?

Harissa is a Tunisian sauce made with puréed chili peppers, cumin and other spices.

THE WALDORF

SERVES 4

FOR SALAD

1 small celeriac, julienned
2 Granny Smith apples, julienned
1/2 cup (125 ml) walnuts, roughly chopped
1/4 cup (60 ml) fresh parsley, chopped

FOR DRESSING

1 egg yolk
2 tbsp lemon juice
1 tbsp Dijon mustard
1/2 cup (125 ml) vegetable oil
1/2 tsp Worcestershire sauce
A few drops Tabasco to taste
Salt and freshly ground pepper

PREPARATION

In a bowl, prepare dressing by whisking together egg yolk, lemon juice, and mustard for 2 minutes. Add oil in a steady stream, whisking vigorously until mixture is creamy. Add Worcestershire, Tabasco and salt and pepper.

In a salad bowl, toss celeriac, apples, walnuts and parsley with dressing. Serve.

TASTY TIP

Satisfy your carnivorous cravings by topping your Waldorf salad with sliced beef!

SAUSAGE SALAD AU GRATIN

SERVES 4

FOR SALAD

4 inches kielbasa sausage, cut into 1/4-inch rounds
1 tbsp vegetable oil
1 red onion, cut into 1-inch cubes
Leaves from 2 sprigs rosemary
1/4 cup (60 ml) balsamic vinegar
2 tbsp olive oil
Salt and freshly ground pepper
1/2 cup (125 ml) cheddar cheese, grated
2 cups (500 ml) baby spinach

PREPARATION

Brown sausage rounds in vegetable oil in a hot oven-safe pan. Add onion and rosemary leaves and cook until golden. Deglaze with balsamic vinegar. Season with olive oil, salt and pepper and sprinkle with grated cheddar cheese. Put pan in the oven and broil until cheese is golden brown. Pile spinach on a serving plate and top with sausage gratin.

DID YOU KNOW?

Kielbasa is a staple of Eastern European cuisine, and there are dozens of different regional varieties including traditional Polish sausage, Hungarian *kolbász* and Ukranian *kovbasa*.

CREAMY COLESLAW

SERVES 4

FOR SALAD

8 cups green cabbage, sliced into very thin ribbons
1 onion, very thinly sliced
2 carrots, peeled and finely julienned

CREAMY MAYONNAISE DRESSING

1/2 cup (125 ml) mayonnaise
1/4 cup (60 ml) vinegar
1 tbsp sugar
1/2 tsp Worcestershire sauce
1 tsp salt
1/2 tsp pepper

PREPARATION

Cook cabbage and onion in a pot of boiling water for 5 seconds. Drain and chill. Set aside.

In a small bowl, combine dressing ingredients.

In a salad bowl, combine cabbage, onion and carrots. Toss with dressing and serve.

TASTY TIP

Serve coleslaw alongside a big, juicy roast chicken leg!

FIESTA OF FRESH HERBS

SERVES 4

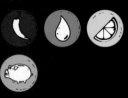

FOR SALAD

Mesclun mix

FOR FRESH HERB VINAIGRETTE

1 cup (250 ml) parsley, chopped with stems
1/2 cup (125 ml) cilantro, chopped with stems
1/3 cup (80 ml) chives, chopped
1 clove garlic
2 tbsp honey
1/4 cup (60 ml) sherry vinegar
1/2 cup (125 ml) canola oil
Salt and pepper
1 tbsp Dijon mustard
1 tbsp wholegrain mustard

PREPARATION

Add herbs and garlic to a pot of boiling water and cook for 30 seconds. Drain and cool.

With a hand blender or in a food processor, combine all vinaigrette ingredients except canola oil. Add oil in a steady stream until fully incorporated.

In a salad bowl, toss mesclun mix with vinaigrette. Serve.

37

WATERMELON FETA CHORIZO

SERVES 4

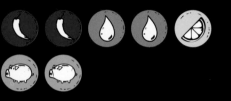

FOR SALAD

1/2 cup (125 ml) cured chorizo, cut into 1/2-inch cubes
2 cups (500 ml) watermelon, seeded and cubed
1 cup (250 ml) feta cheese, cubed or crumbled
1/3 cup (80 ml) fresh mint, chopped
1 cup (250 ml) arugula, roughly chopped
1 Thai chili, minced
1/2 red onion, finely chopped

FOR VINAIGRETTE

2 tbsp olive oil
2 tbsp lemon juice
1/2 tsp salt

PREPARATION

In a pan, fry chorizo for 2 to 3 minutes until edges are crisp. Pat chorizo dry with a paper towel to soak up excess oil.

In a salad bowl, combine all salad ingredients with vinaigrette ingredients.

DID YOU KNOW?

Chorizo is a spicy cured or fresh sausage from Spain or Latin America. Both types are widely available in most major North American grocery stores.

38

DUCK CONFIT & GOAT CHEESE

SERVES 4

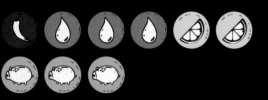

FOR SALAD

4 slices fresh plain goat cheese
1/4 cup (60 ml) flour
2 eggs
1/2 cup (125 ml) panko (Japanese bread crumbs)
2 tbsp vegetable oil
2 confit duck legs, skin removed, meat shredded
into bite-sized pieces
3 cups (750 ml) mesclun mix
4 fresh figs, cut into 6

FOR NUT VINAIGRETTE

2 shallots, minced
2 tbsp walnut oil
1/4 cup (60 ml) olive oil
2 tbsp honey
3 tbsp sherry vinegar
1 tsp Chinese five-spice

PREPARATION

Coat goat cheese rounds with flour, dip in egg and then coat with panko. Dip in egg and panko again to form a crust that will hold during cooking. In a pan, heat oil and fry cheese until golden brown on both sides, then cook in a 350°F (180°C) oven for 5 minutes. Set aside.

Heat duck in the microwave for 20 seconds. Set aside. In a small bowl, mix together vinaigrette ingredients.

In a salad bowl, combine mesclun and figs and toss with vinaigrette. Gently stir in shredded duck. Top each salad serving with a goat cheese round.

 **DID YOU KNOW?**

Chinese five-spice powder is a blend of Sichuan pepper, star anise, cinnamon, cloves, and fennel seeds.

39

MEDITERRANEAN CHEESE & TAPENADE

SERVES 4

FOR SALAD

4 slices halloumi cheese
3 tbsp olive oil
2 cups (500 ml) eggplant, cut into 1/2-inch cubes
2 pitas, toasted and cut into slices
12 cherry tomatoes, quartered

FOR OLIVE TAPENADE

1/4 cup (60 ml) Kalamata olives, rinsed and pitted
1 tbsp capers, rinsed and pitted
1/2 clove garlic or 1 tbsp garlic confit
(see recipe for garlic confit page 172)
2 tbsp fresh oregano, chopped
2 tbsp olive oil

PREPARATION

Desalt halloumi cheese by placing slices in a bowl and running cold water over them for 2 minutes. In a non-stick pan, fry halloumi over medium-high heat in 1 tbsp olive oil for 30 seconds. Heat 2 tbsp olive oil in a pan and cook eggplant for 4 minutes or until tender. Set aside.

With a hand blender or in a food processor, purée olives, capers, garlic or confit, oregano and olive oil. In a salad bowl, toss eggplant and tomatoes with olive tapenade. Arrange hot halloumi slices on a serving plate, top with salad, and serve with pita.

DID YOU KNOW?

Halloumi is a firm, salty cheese from Cyprus, an island in the Mediterranean Sea. This cheese is traditionally made from goat's milk and sheep's milk, but can also be made from cow's milk.

SCANDINAVIAN SALAD

SERVES 4

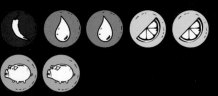

FOR SALAD

2 medium yellow beets
8 new potatoes, unpeeled
6 quail eggs
2 dill pickles, thinly sliced
1/2 red onion, finely chopped
3 fillets smoked herring in oil, drained and cut into four pieces

FOR HORSERADISH SOUR CREAM

1/2 cup (125 ml) sour cream
1 tbsp chives
1 tsp horseradish
Salt and freshly ground pepper

FOR VINAIGRETTE

1 tbsp Pommery mustard (or wholegrain mustard)
2 tbsp olive oil
1 tbsp lemon juice
Salt and freshly ground pepper

PREPARATION

Fill a pot with water. Add beets and salt and bring to a boil. Cook until beets are tender and easily pierced with a knife. Drain and cool, then peel and thinly slice. Repeat with potatoes, but cut potatoes into quarters. Cook quail eggs in salted water for 4 minutes. Immediately place in cold water. When cool, peel and cut each egg in half.

In a small bowl, mix together sour cream, chives and horseradish. Season.

In a large salad bowl, combine salad ingredients except herring and toss with vinaigrette. Plate salads and top each serving with smoked herring and 1 tbsp horseradish sour cream.

DID YOU KNOW?

Horseradish is often served with roast beef and is a common ingredient in savory cocktails and shrimp cocktail sauce.

WILD RICE SALAD

SERVES 4

FOR SALAD

1 cup (250 ml) wild rice, cooked
2 cups (500 ml) butternut squash, peeled and cubed
1 tbsp olive oil
1/2 cup (125 ml) bacon
1/4 cup (60 ml) shelled, toasted pumpkin seeds
2 tbsp fresh tarragon, chopped
1 cup (250 ml) red-skinned apple, diced

FOR VINAIGRETTE

1 tbsp bacon fat
1 tbsp Dijon mustard
2 tbsp red wine vinegar
1/4 cup (60 ml) olive oil

PREPARATION

Cook wild rice according to package directions.

Toss cubed butternut squash with olive oil and spread evenly on a baking sheet covered with parchment paper. Cook in a 400°F (200°C) oven for 30 minutes or until squash is easily pierced with a knife.

Cook bacon in a pan. Reserve 1 tbsp bacon fat for vinaigrette.

In a small bowl, whisk together vinaigrette ingredients. In a salad bowl, toss salad ingredients with vinaigrette. Serve.

42

CURRIED LENTIL SALAD

SERVES 4

FOR SALAD

1 cup (250 ml) lentils, cooked *al dente*
2 tomatoes, diced
1 carrot, diced
2 celery sticks, finely chopped
1 shallot, finely chopped
2 cups (500 ml) baby spinach, roughly chopped

FOR YOGURT CURRY DRESSING

1/2 cup (125 ml) plain yogurt
2 tbsp olive oil
1 tbsp yellow curry paste
1 tsp sugar
1 tbsp lemon juice

PREPARATION

In a small bowl, combine dressing ingredients. In a salad bowl, mix together salad ingredients and toss with dressing. Serve.

43

LA REMOULADE

SERVES 4

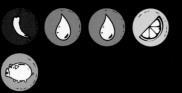

FOR SALAD

1 medium celeriac, julienned
1/2 cup mayonnaise
2 tbsp pickles, finely chopped
2 tbsp capers, drained, rinsed, and finely chopped
2 tbsp fresh tarragon, finely chopped
2 tbsp fresh chives, finely chopped
2 tbsp fresh parsley, finely chopped
1 tbsp Dijon mustard
1 tbsp lemon juice
1 tbsp 15% cream

PREPARATION

In a salad bowl, mix together all salad ingredients. Chill for 2 hours and serve.

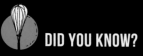 DID YOU KNOW?

Remoulade is a mayonnaise-based French sauce that is also very popular in Denmark and Louisiana.

44

INDONESIAN GADO-GADO

SERVES 4

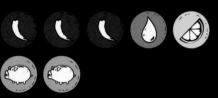

FOR GADO-GADO SAUCE

1 tbsp vegetable oil
2/3 cup (160 ml) peanuts
2 shallots, minced
1 clove garlic, minced
2 Thai chili peppers, seeded and minced
1 tsp shrimp paste
1/2 cup (125 ml) coconut milk
1 tbsp brown sugar

FOR SALAD

1/2 cucumber, cut into sticks
1 handful bean sprouts
2 hard-boiled eggs, cut into quarters
A few romaine lettuce leaves
10 green beans, blanched
2 carrots, cut into sticks and blanched
A few slices of tofu, fried
1 cup (250 ml) fresh cilantro
Shrimp chips (krupuk)

PREPARATION

To prepare gado-gado sauce, heat vegetable oil in a pan and toast peanuts. Grind in a food processor and add remaining sauce ingredients. Purée until smooth. Add water if sauce is too thick.

Arrange salad ingredients on a serving platter and serve with a bowl of gado-gado sauce on the side.

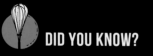

DID YOU KNOW?

Gado-gado is a traditional Indonesian specialty famous for its spicy peanut sauce.

SHRIMP & SOBA

SERVES 4

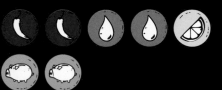

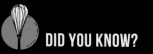 **DID YOU KNOW?**

Historians believe that soba noodles, which are made from buckwheat flour and water, first appeared in the 16th century. Soba, udon and ramen noodles are now considered a staple food across Japan.

FOR MARINADE

2 tbsp soy sauce
1 tsp fish sauce
1 tbsp honey

FOR SALAD

16 large shrimp, peeled
2 servings soba noodles (plain or green tea), cooked and drained
1 carrot, julienned
1 zucchini, julienned
2 green onions, thinly sliced
1/2 cup (125 ml) fresh cilantro, chopped

FOR GINGER LEMONGRASS MAYONNAISE

2 tbsp mayonnaise
1 Thai chili pepper, seeded and minced
1 tsp lemongrass, chopped
2 tbsp ginger, minced
Juice of 1/2 lime
1 tbsp soy sauce
1 tbsp honey

PREPARATION

Toss shrimp with marinade ingredients. Marinate for 2 hours. Thread shrimp onto skewers and grill for 2 minutes each side.

In a small bowl, mix together mayonnaise ingredients.

In a salad bowl, combine noodles, carrot, zucchini, green onion and cilantro and toss with vinaigrette. Serve shrimp skewers on a bed of salad.

46

SAUTÉED DUCK WITH BLUE CHEESE DRESSING

SERVES 4

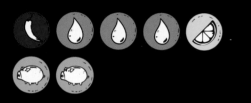

FOR SALAD

2 tbsp duck fat (or butter)
2 new potatoes, sliced
1 onion, sliced
12 confit duck gizzards
2 tbsp white wine
2 cups (500 ml) mâche (or baby spinach)
12 cherry tomatoes, halved

FOR BLUE CHEESE DRESSING

1/2 cup (125 ml) mayonnaise
1 clove garlic, minced
1/4 cup (60 ml) chives, finely chopped
1/4 cup (60 ml) sour cream
1/4 cup (60 ml) blue cheese, crumbled
1 tbsp white wine vinegar
Salt and freshly ground pepper

PREPARATION

In a large pan, heat duck fat and cook potatoes until golden brown. Add onion and cook until golden. Add gizzards and deglaze with white wine. Cover and cook for 6 minutes or until potatoes are easily pierced with a knife.

In a small bowl, combine dressing ingredients.

On a serving plate, arrange gizzards on top of potatoes and onions, mâche, and tomatoes. Drizzle dressing over salad.

47

GRANDMA'S MACARONI SALAD

SERVES 4

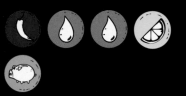

FOR SMOKED PAPRIKA AIOLI

1 egg yolk
1 tbsp lemon juice
1 tsp Dijon mustard
1 clove garlic, minced
1/2 cup (125 ml) canola oil
1/2 tsp smoked paprika
Salt and freshly ground pepper

FOR SALAD

1 cup macaroni or other small pasta, cooked *al dente*
1 cup cooked ham, diced
2 celery sticks, diced
1 cup (250 ml) fresh corn
1/4 cup parsley, chopped

PREPARATION

In a bowl, prepare aioli by whisking together the egg yolk, lemon juice, mustard and garlic. Add oil in a steady stream, whisking vigorously until mixture is creamy. Season with smoked paprika, salt and pepper.

In a salad bowl, combine salad ingredients. Toss with aioli and serve.

48

GRILLED VEGGIES WITH ROASTED SQUASH

SERVES 4

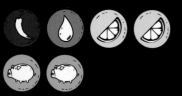

FOR SALAD

2 cups (500 ml) butternut squash, peeled and cut into large cubes
1/4 cup (60 ml) olive oil
Salt and freshly ground pepper
2 portobello mushrooms, thickly sliced
2 zucchinis, cut lengthwise into thin slices
1 red onion, quartered
2 red peppers, seeded and cut into thick slices
1/2 radicchio, thinly sliced

FOR OREGANO VINAIGRETTE

1/4 cup (60 ml) olive oil
3 tbsp balsamic vinegar
1/4 cup (60 ml) fresh oregano, chopped
Salt and pepper

PREPARATION

In a bowl, mix together cubed squash, salt and pepper with 2 tbsp olive oil. Spread mixture evenly on a baking sheet covered with parchment paper and roast in a 400°F (200°C) oven for 20 minutes or until squash is easily pierced with a knife. Set aside.

In a large bowl, toss portobellos, zucchini, red onion and red peppers with 2 tbsp olive oil. Grill vegetables in a grill pan with a ridged surface or on the barbecue until slightly charred.

In a small bowl, combine vinaigrette ingredients. In a salad bowl, gently toss roasted squash, grilled vegetables, and radicchio with vinaigrette. Serve.

TASTY TIP

This is a great side dish to accompany grilled meats!

49

AWESOME ASPARAGUS & PARM

SERVES 4

FOR SALAD

10 green asparagus spears
2 tbsp butter
2 cups country bread, cut into large cubes
1 tbsp olive oil
2 cloves garlic, minced
1/2 leek, thinly sliced
2 tbsp lemon juice
Parmesan shavings, to taste
1 tsp sea salt
Freshly ground pepper

PREPARATION

Blanch asparagus for 1 minute in a large pot of boiling salted water. Plunge immediately into a bowl of ice water to preserve color. Drain and cut in half lengthwise.

In a pan, heat 1 tbsp butter and sauté bread until golden. Add olive oil, garlic and leek and cook until tender. Remove from heat. Add lemon juice and remaining butter and toss gently until butter is melted. Pour mixture over asparagus in a serving dish. Garnish with Parmesan shavings, sea salt, and freshly ground pepper.

LA PANZANELLA

SERVES 4

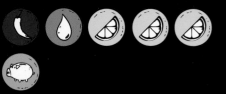

FOR SALAD

3 tbsp red wine vinegar
1/4 cup (60 ml) olive oil
2 small loaves ciabatta, torn into bite-sized pieces
2 tomatoes, quartered
1 red onion, finely chopped
1/2 cucumber, diced
1/4 cup (60 ml) fresh oregano, chopped
A few fresh basil leaves, chopped

PREPARATION

In a salad bowl, combine vinegar and olive oil. Add bread, mix together, and let soak in mixture until moistened. Toss with other ingredients and serve.

DID YOU KNOW?

Panzanella is a classic Tuscan bread salad. Because it doesn't require cooking, it's often served as a light, fresh summer dish or as a simple starter.

TROUT WITH CARAMELIZED PECANS

SERVES 4

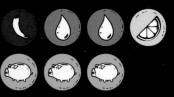

FOR SALAD

1 tbsp butter
4 small boneless trout fillets
2 cups (500 ml) baby spinach

FOR CARAMELIZED PECANS

1 cup (250 ml) pecans
2 tbsp maple syrup (or honey)
1/2 tsp salt
2 tbsp icing sugar
1 tsp lemon juice

FOR MAPLE VINAIGRETTE

1 tbsp wholegrain mustard
2 tbsp maple syrup (or honey)
1/4 cup (60 ml) balsamic vinegar
1/3 cup (80 ml) olive oil
Salt and freshly ground pepper

PREPARATION

In a non-stick pan, heat butter and cook trout for 2 minutes on each side or until fish flakes easily with a fork. Reserve.

In a bowl, combine pecans, maple syrup, salt, icing sugar and lemon juice. Spread pecans evenly on a baking sheet covered with parchment paper. Bake for 10 minutes in a 300°F (150°C) oven. Cool completely before adding to salad.

In a small bowl, prepare vinaigrette by whisking together mustard, maple syrup, vinegar, and salt and pepper. Add oil in a steady stream, whisking vigorously until mixture is smooth.

In a salad bowl, toss spinach with vinaigrette. On a serving plate, arrange trout on a bed of spinach. Drizzle with more vinaigrette and sprinkle with caramelized pecans.

CHICKPEA, MUSHROOM & FETA

SERVES 4

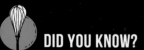

DID YOU KNOW?

Ras el hanout is a blend of spices used across North Africa. It typically includes cinnamon, cardamom, nutmeg, clove, turmeric, ginger, and cumin.

FOR SALAD

1/4 cup (60 ml) olive oil
1 clove garlic, minced
12 button mushrooms, cut into quarters
2 cups (500 ml) eggplant, diced
2 tomatoes, diced
1 tsp Ras el hanout
1/4 cup (60 ml) white wine
Juice of 1/2 lemon
1 cup (250 ml) canned chickpeas, drained and rinsed
1/2 cup (125 ml) feta cheese, crumbled
1/4 cup (60 ml) cilantro, chopped
2 tbsp fresh mint, chopped

PREPARATION

In a pan, heat 2 tbsp olive oil and sauté garlic, mushrooms and eggplant until tender. Add tomatoes, Ras el hanout, white wine, and lemon juice and cook for 2 minutes until warmed through.

In a salad bowl, toss cooked vegetables with chickpeas, feta cheese, fresh herbs, and remaining olive oil. Serve.

53

CUCUMBER WAKAME

SERVES 4

TASTY TIP

Wakame salad makes an excellent side dish for seafood, marinated tofu, or even sushi!

DID YOU KNOW?

Wakame is an edible sea vegetable widely used in Japanese and Korean cuisine.

FOR JAPANESE VINAIGRETTE

1 tsp sesame oil
1/3 cup (80 ml) rice vinegar
1 tbsp Japanese soy sauce
1 tsp sugar

FOR SALAD

1/2 cup (125 ml) dried wakame
2 small cucumbers, julienned
1 carrot, julienned
2 tbsp fresh ginger, minced
1 tbsp white (or black) sesame seeds
1 fresh Thai chili, seeded and finely minced

PREPARATION

In a small bowl, combine Japanese vinaigrette ingredients. Stir until sugar is dissolved.

Soak wakame for 10 minutes in a large bowl filled with cold water. Drain well and set aside.

In a salad bowl, mix together wakame, cucumber and carrot. Toss with vinaigrette, ginger, sesame seeds, and minced chili. Serve.

GUILTY PLEASURE

SERVES 4

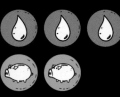

54

FOR CHOCOLATE SAUCE

1/2 cup (125 ml) 15% cream
1/2 cup (125 ml) Nutella

FOR SALAD

2 grapefruits, peeled and sectioned,
pith and membranes removed
2 tbsp grapefruit juice
1 apple or pear, thinly sliced
1 cup (250 ml) red grapes
1 banana, sliced
1 cup (250 ml) whole raspberries
1/2 cup (125 ml) sliced toasted almonds
1 tbsp icing sugar

PREPARATION

In a small pot, whisk together cream and Nutella until melted. Set aside.

In a salad bowl, mix together salad ingredients. Serve chocolate sauce on the side.

55

WESTERN CHICKEN SALAD

SERVES 4

FOR MARINADE

2 chicken breasts, cut in half lengthwise
1 onion, chopped
1 tsp paprika
1 tsp harissa
Juice of 1/2 lemon
2 cloves garlic, crushed
1/2 chicken bouillon cube
2 sprigs fresh thyme, chopped
Freshly ground pepper

FOR RANCH DRESSING

1/2 cup (125 ml) mayonnaise
1/4 cup (60 ml) sour cream
2 tbsp fresh chives, finely chopped
2 tbsp fresh dill, finely chopped
1/2 tsp garlic powder
1 tsp onion powder
1 tbsp water
Salt and freshly ground pepper

FOR BATTER

1 tsp mild paprika
2 tbsp Parmesan cheese
1/4 cup (60 ml) Italian bread crumbs
1/4 cup (60 ml) flour
1 egg

PREPARATION

Mix together all marinade ingredients. Coat chicken in mixture and marinate for at least 4 hours.

In a small bowl, combine dressing ingredients. Refrigerate for 30 minutes.

In a bowl, combine paprika, Parmesan cheese, and bread crumbs. When the chicken has finished marinating, dredge in flour, dip in egg, and coat in bread crumbs. Heat oil in a pan and fry chicken for 5 to 7 minutes on each side until fully cooked and batter is crispy. If pieces are not fully cooked through, finish in the oven at 350°F (180°C).

In a bowl, mix together chopped lettuce, tomato, cucumber, and onion (or any combination of salad fixings) and toss with ranch dressing. Serve chicken on a bed of salad garnished with a drizzle of ranch dressing.

56

BABY SCALLOPS WITH POLENTA

SERVES 4

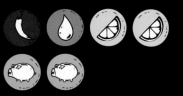

FOR ROSEMARY POLENTA

1 tbsp olive oil
1 shallot, minced
2 tbsp fresh rosemary, chopped
1/4 cup (60 ml) white wine
1 cup (250 ml) milk
1/2 cup (125 ml) instant polenta
1 tbsp butter

FOR SALAD

1 tbsp olive oil
1 cup (250 ml) small scallops
4 canned artichoke hearts, drained and cut into quarters
2 grapefruits, peeled and sectioned,
pith and membranes removed
1 cup (250 ml) canned or frozen shelled edamame,
rinsed and drained

FOR GRAPEFRUIT VINAIGRETTE

1/4 cup (60 ml) olive oil
1 tbsp rice vinegar
2 tbsp grapefruit juice
A few drops sriracha sauce

PREPARATION

To prepare polenta, heat olive oil in a small pan. Sauté shallot and rosemary. Deglaze with white wine, add milk, and bring to a boil. Reduce heat and gradually add polenta, whisking constantly to prevent lumps from forming. Cook for 2 minutes. To set polenta, pour into a baking dish lined with parchment paper, spreading evenly until it is 1/2-inch thick. Chill for 30 minutes.

In a non-stick pan, heat 1 tbsp olive oil and sear scallops with artichokes. Set aside.

When polenta has set and cooled, remove from pan and slice into small squares. In a pan, melt butter and fry polenta until golden brown.

In a small bowl, combine vinaigrette ingredients. In a salad bowl, mix together salad ingredients and toss with vinaigrette and polenta squares. Serve.

CARIBBEAN DELIGHT

SERVES 4

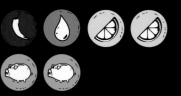

57

FOR GINGER SYRUP

1/2 cup (125 ml) brown sugar
1-inch piece ginger, minced
Juice and zest of 2 limes

FOR SALAD

2 mangoes, peeled and cubed
1 star fruit, sliced
2 cups (500 ml) pineapple, cubed
3 kiwis, peeled and cubed

PREPARATION

In a small pot, heat ginger syrup ingredients and boil for 1 minute. Chill and set aside.

In a salad bowl, toss salad ingredients with syrup. Serve.

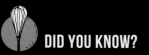

DID YOU KNOW?

Star fruit is another name for the carambola, a ridged fruit that is thought to have originated in Sri Lanka or in Indonesia's Malaku Islands and has been cultivated in parts of Asia for hundreds of years.

58

CALIFORNIA PORK SALAD

SERVES 4

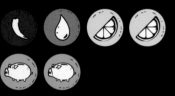

FOR SALAD

1 pork loin
Salt and freshly ground pepper
1 tbsp vegetable oil
1/4 cup (60 ml) Asian sweet-and-sour sauce
1 head romaine lettuce, grilled
1/2 cup (125 ml) pecans, toasted
4 clementines, peeled and sectioned,
pith and membranes removed
1 red pepper, sliced into thin strips
1 tbsp white sesame seeds

FOR CLEMENTINE VINAIGRETTE

1/4 cup (60 ml) olive oil
1 tbsp red wine vinegar
2 tbsp clementine juice
1 tsp sesame oil
Salt and freshly ground pepper

PREPARATION

Season pork loin with salt and pepper and sear on each side in an oiled pan. Heat oven to 350°F (180°C) and cook for 8 minutes. Remove pork from oven, thinly slice, and coat with sweet-and-sour sauce. Set aside.

In a small bowl, combine vinaigrette ingredients.

To grill romaine lettuce, separate exterior leaves and keep the heart whole. Brush with a bit of vegetable oil. Grill lettuce in a grill pan with a ridged surface or on the barbecue for a few minutes until it softens and becomes slightly charred. Set aside.

Arrange grilled romaine on a serving platter along with pecans, clementines and red pepper. Top with sliced pork, drizzle generously with vinaigrette, and garnish with sesame seeds.

59

OODLES OF OCTOPUS

SERVES 4

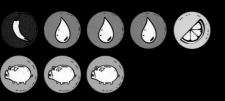

FOR SALAD

2 octopus tentacles (about 1 lb)
1 onion
1 bay leaf
1 tbsp black peppercorns
2 cloves garlic, crushed
1/2 cup (125 ml) green lentils
1/4 cup (60 ml) chives, finely chopped
3 shallots, finely chopped and fried (see recipe page 036)

FOR TOMATO CONFIT

1/4 cup (60 ml) olive oil
4 Italian tomatoes, halved
1 sprig fresh rosemary
4 sprigs fresh thyme
2 cloves garlic, sliced
2 tbsp sugar
Salt and freshly ground pepper

FOR BASIL MAYONNAISE

1/4 cup (60 ml) fresh basil, finely chopped
Juice of 1 lemon
2 tbsp mayonnaise

PREPARATION

Place octopus, onion, bay leaf, black pepper, and garlic in a pot of water and bring to a boil. Reduce heat and simmer for 1 hour. Remove tentacles and chill for a few minutes before slicing into 1/4-inch rounds.

In another pot, add lentils to salted water and bring to a boil. Cook for 20 minutes or until lentils are tender.

In a bowl, combine oil, tomatoes, rosemary and thyme sprigs, garlic, sugar, salt and pepper. Spread mixture evenly on a baking sheet, cut sides up. Roast in a 300°F (180°C) oven for 2 hours.

With a hand blender or in a food processor, combine basil, lemon juice and mayonnaise. In a salad bowl, mix together octopus, lentils, chives, fried shallots, tomatoes and basil mayonnaise. Serve.

RED PEPPER & HEARTS OF PALM

SERVES 4

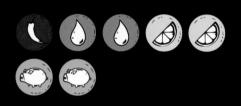

FOR SALAD

3 red peppers (or yellow or orange peppers)
1 tbsp vegetable oil
2 cups tortellini, cooked
2/3 cup (160 ml) hearts of palm, thinly sliced
1/4 cup (60 ml) fresh oregano, chopped

FOR GARLIC CONFIT

4 whole garlic bulbs
1/4 cup (60 ml) olive oil
Salt and freshly ground pepper

FOR GARLIC CONFIT VINAIGRETTE

3 tbsp mayonnaise
1 tbsp garlic confit
1 tbsp balsamic vinegar

PREPARATION

Brush peppers with oil and place on a baking sheet. Broil for 5 minutes on each side or until skin blackens and is easy to remove. Place in a bowl, cover, and allow to cool. Remove skin, stems and seeds and slice into thin strips. Set aside.

To make the garlic confit, cut off and discard garlic tips and bases. Place bulbs on a baking sheet, base side down. Pour olive oil over bulbs and season with salt and pepper. Roast in a 300°F (150°C) oven for 40 minutes. When garlic is golden brown, remove from oven and allow to cool. Peel skin off cloves and purée with a hand blender or in a food processor. In a small bowl, whisk together garlic confit, mayonnaise and balsamic vinegar.

In a salad bowl, combine roasted peppers, cooked tortellini, hearts of palm and oregano. Toss with vinaigrette and serve.

 **DID YOU KNOW?**

When preserved in olive oil, roasted peppers and garlic confit will keep for several weeks in the refrigerator.

INGREDIENTS INDEX

VINAIGRETTES, DRESSINGS, MARINADES AND SAUCES

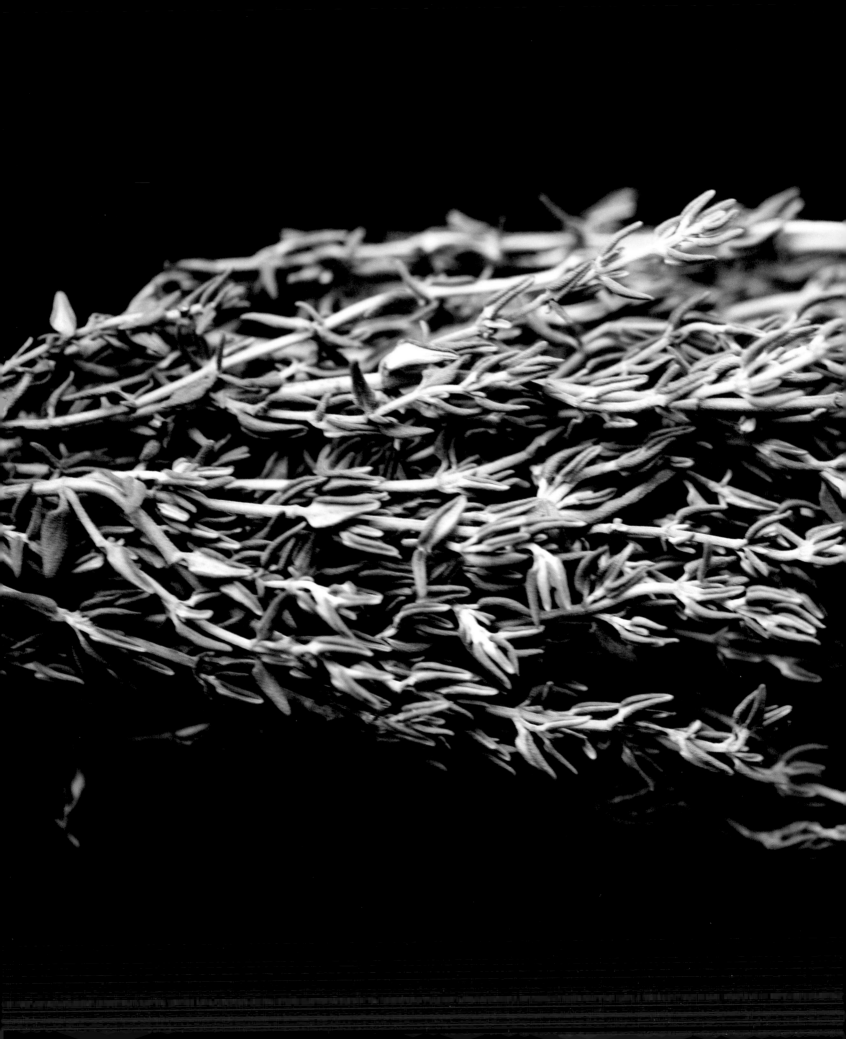

CONVERSION CHART

1 dl	10 cl	100 ml
1 tablespoon		15 ml
1 teaspoon		5 ml
1 oz.		30 ml
1 cup		250 ml
4 cups		1 l
1/2 cup		125 ml
1/4 cup		60 ml
1/3 cup		80 ml
1 lb		450 g
2 lbs		900 g
2.2 lbs		1 kg
400°F	200°C	T/7
350°F	175°C	T/6
300°F	150°C	T/5

Volume Conversion
* Approximate values

---

1 cup (250 ml) crumbled cheese	150 g
1 cup (250 ml) all-purpose flour	115 g
1 cup (250 ml) white sugar	200 g
1 cup (250 ml) brown sugar	220 g
1 cup (250 ml) butter	230 g
1 cup (250 ml) oil	215 g
1 cup (250 ml) canned tomatoes	250 g

NOTES

60

IN THE SAME COLLECTION

THE WORLD'S 60 BEST
BURGERS
PERIOD.

THE WORLD'S 60 BEST
PASTA SAUCES
PERIOD.